Komodo Dragons

by Cari Meister

Bullfrog Books

Ideas for Parents and Teachers

Bullfrog Books let children practice reading informational text at the earliest reading levels. Repetition, familiar words, and photo labels support early readers.

Before Reading

• Discuss the cover photo. What does it tell them?

• Look at the picture glossary together. Read and discuss the words.

Read the Book

• "Walk" through the book and look at the photos. Let the child ask questions. Point out the photo labels.

• Read the book to the child, or have him or her read independently.

After Reading

• Prompt the child to think more. Ask: Have you ever seen a Komodo dragon? Did it look like you would imagine a dragon to look?

Bullfrog Books are published by Jump!
5357 Penn Avenue South
Minneapolis, MN 55419
www.jumplibrary.com

Library of Congress Cataloging-in-Publication Data

Meister, Cari, author.
  Komodo dragons / by Cari Meister.
    Pages cm. — (Bullfrog books. Reptile world)
  Summary: "This photo-illustrated book for beginning readers describes the physical features and behaviors of Komodo dragons. Includes picture glossary and index."—Provided by publisher.
  Audience: Ages 5–8.
  Audience: K to grade 3.
  Includes index.
  ISBN 978-1-62031-197-4 (hardcover: alk. paper) —
  ISBN 978-1-62496-284-4 (ebook)
  1. Komodo dragon—Juvenile literature. I. Title.
  QL666.L29M45 2016
  597.95'968—dc23
                                    2014042731

Editor: Jenny Fretland VanVoorst
Series Designer: Ellen Huber
Book Designer: Lindaanne Donohoe
Photo Researcher: Jenny Fretland VanVoorst

Photo Credits: All photos by Shutterstock except: age fotostock, 6–7; Alamy, 4, 10–11; iStock, cover; Juniors Bildarchiv, 15; Nature Picture Library, 9; SuperStock, 16–17; Thinkstock, 8.

Printed in the United States of America at Corporate Graphics in North Mankato, Minnesota.

To Aidan—JFV

Table of Contents

A Big Lizard

A Komodo dragon
is not a dragon.

He is a lizard.

But he is very like a dragon.

5

Look how big he is!
He is 10 feet
(3 meters) long.

His skin has scales.

Do you see his tongue?

It is long.

It is forked.

The Komodo dragon
is strong.

He runs.

He swims.

He fights.

He climbs.

13

Look at his mouth!

He has venom.

14

He bites.

His prey dies.

Do you see his claws?

They rip.

Time to eat!
He swallows
big chunks.

He does
not chew.

Now he is full.

It is time to sleep!

Parts of a Komodo Dragon

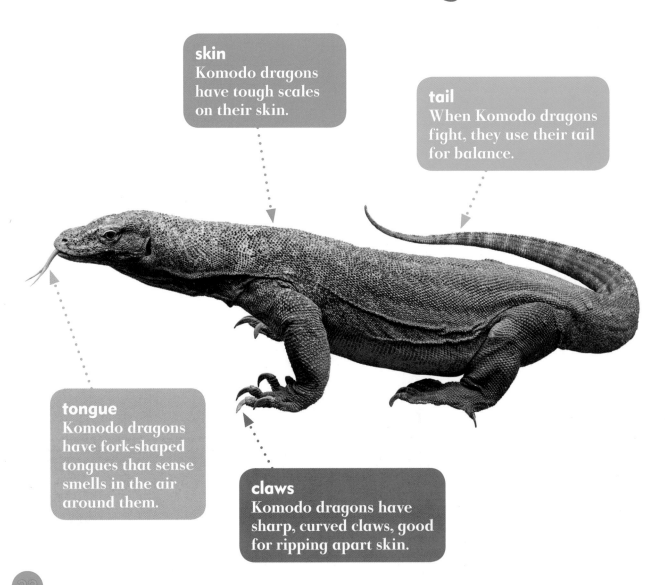

skin
Komodo dragons have tough scales on their skin.

tail
When Komodo dragons fight, they use their tail for balance.

tongue
Komodo dragons have fork-shaped tongues that sense smells in the air around them.

claws
Komodo dragons have sharp, curved claws, good for ripping apart skin.

Picture Glossary

dragon
An imaginary animal usually pictured as a lizard with wings and large claws.

scales
Strong plates that protect a lizard's body.

prey
Animals that are hunted for food.

venom
Poison.

Index

To Learn More

Learning more is as easy as 1, 2, 3.

1) Go to www.factsurfer.com

2) Enter "Komododragons" into the search box.

3) Click the "Surf" button to see a list of websites.

With factsurfer.com, finding more information is just a click away.